Christmas in Africa

By the same author

Twelve to Twelve (ed)
Flying
Monkeys' Wedding
The Happiness Bird

Christmas in Africa

Jeni Couzyn

HEINEMANN
LONDON

J. J. DOUGLAS
VANCOUVER

Heinemann Educational Books Ltd
LONDON EDINBURGH MELBOURNE AUCKLAND TORONTO
HONG KONG SINGAPORE KUALA LUMPUR NEW DELHI
NAIROBI JOHANNESBURG LUSAKA IBADAN
KINGSTON

ISBN (U.K.) 0 435 14180 5
ISBN (CANADA) 0-88894-096-3

First published 1975
Reprinted 1977

Published by
Heinemann Educational Books Ltd, 48 Charles Street,
London W1 and J. J. Douglas Ltd, 3645 McKechnie Drive,
West Vancouver, British Columbia

Type Set by Malvern Typesetting Services and
Printed in Great Britain by
Biddles of Guildford, Martyr Road, Guildford, Surrey

Acknowledgements

Christmas in Africa was originally published in Bangla Desh, translated into Bengali by Syed Shamsul Haq. It was first broadcast on Radio 3, and first published in English in the *Malahat Review* by Robin Skelton.

All the poems in the second section of the book have been published in Foundation, and, with the exception of the two giant poems, are based on stories by Brian Aldiss. Some of the poems, like 'Inside Outside', use the idea of the story as a starting point only for the poem, others, like 'Marapper the Priest', try to be as faithful as possible to the images and vocabulary. All the poems take the central image of the story and expand it, treating it in a symbolic way to make my own personal statement. My thanks to Brian Aldiss and other science fiction writers who constantly tug and stretch my brain.

My thanks are also due to *Workshop, Poetry Now, Books,* published by the National Book League, *Peace News, Beyond This Horizon, Gallery, Vogue* and *Izwi*, where some of these poems have previously appeared.

for Jafar
dowser
lighthouse keeper

Contents

I
Christmas in Africa

1. In The House Of The Father

Christmas, the turning time, the final reckoning and the
forgiveness, we rode towards each year, over humps of
bitterness, towards the father

omnipotent and bountiful night rider with his magical
reindeer and sack full of gifts —
you could rely on him always to be there when you got there

accept the culmination of your year in his lap
hear all, forgive with a wish, and let you
begin all over;

a time of reprieve and new resolutions, time when you could
believe in new beginnings, a time of peace and long
playtime. With a hand in the dark

it began before dawn. The sun would rise over the city
as we passed the last gold hills of the mine dumps. Always
I saw children leaping up them, and in my head, in
golden depths

a heap of little skeletons. Then the long hot hours
through the karroo
through the dorps each its single tree and tin roofs blazing
each its lone dog barking and black silent men

propped on the verandah of the general store, drinking
lemonade. Endless car games, the singing game chanting
every rhyme we knew
from ten green bottles to jesus loves me over the veld

to pass the time. At last, crossing, purple and lonely
the valley of a thousand hills, the tropical
deep smell of heavy flowers would glut the evening

and my father offered sixpence for the first to see the sea.
And there it was after a sudden unbending—that immense
blue promise.
Then inland into the sugar cane in the deep of night

the rustle of dunes and the sugar cane fields
the farmers who kept pythons fifty feet long to keep the
rats down
and at midnight

the cottage. O the damp smell of foliage, smell of salt
and the sea's heavy breathing in the night, stray cries
of live things, batswing, shadow, sleep, and a ring of mornings.

The snakes were the price. In their hundreds they inhabited
our world at christmas. They were the hazard
in the garden. And they were everywhere

tangled in undergrowth, slithering over your feet in the pathway
stretched across doorways in the sun
lurking under the banana plant and nesting in the
luckybean tree

they were everywhere, everywhere. And happiness was
everywhere
in the father's time, who came down from heaven
in his red dressing gown and my father's shoes at the
appointed time

cottonwool beard lobsided across his grin
his arms full of parcels.
His was the future that always came, keeping its promise.

In the house of the father the year would turn
a flower full blown, shedding its petals.
Glistened in your hand a free gift, a clean seed.

2. The Garden

The sun has its season. Under the ocean's strong shoulder
all was a wild growing, a richness of green
shimmering and brooding.

Here we cut back the marulla hedges and fleshy leaves each year
cleared a gap in the dense green
where sometimes at dawn wild monkeys and deer

would peer from the foliage and take
fruit from our hands.
Here when they were young my parents built a house

a refuge, a wild place for their love to thrive in
and dreamed of a son. Here my father
hoisted the beams, raised brave walls against the world

laid a fine roof with his strong arms against rain
and beside the kitchen door in fresh concrete
he dipped our feet. Three tiny footprints

sealed there through all the stark years
never changing. On the forest floor a corridor of leaves
wound secretly to the inland track we used as a road

and therc the fruitsellars came
with their green load to the shore, two huge baskets
on the ends of a pole

strung over the shoulder, pawpaw and grenadillas
huge bunches of green bananas that hung from ceiling to floor
as they ripened

sponspec and mangoes, lychees and sugar cane.
They would whistle for us at the door each day and my mother
never sent them away.

From the verandah my father built a pathway
winding through a hump of green forest
to a high bank. And there

the sea suddenly opened below you, flew out
with sky and the clean white beach welcoming
heavy booming of breakers

calling and calling—
a richness of blue that filled the wide hole in the world
with sun and water.

There he built a concrete staircase
that dropped like a rock to the beach and as you plunged
downward
a million green hands

reached out and clutched you.
At dawn the sand was pure white, untouched and warm
and I wandered between water and land

nesting in the rock pools
with crabs and little quick fish, gathering cowries and popping
black bubbles of seaweed –

searched for sea-urchins, jellyfish, starfish and cuttlefish
that were laid out along the high water mark each morning
in a new ribbon

always I went alone. For love is an opening, an outward thing
but the need for love is a hunger that no food will fill
and though you grip your limbs around you

build your house in a green cavern
yet in yawns in you wide
as an ocean storm.

And so I gave myself to the sea then
and it sang
its full song in me.

3. The Punishment

One autumn afternoon when I was nine
feeding the chickens near the grapevine, brooding
in sunshine, my mother asked me to choose

a christmas present that year.
Anything I said, but a doll. Whatever you choose
but not a doll

my faith in her to know
better than I could myself what gift would please me.
And so at the height of summer

we made our pilgrimage
to the earth's greenest riches and the ample ocean.
And christmas eve

was three white daughters
three bright angels singing silent night as my mother
lit the candles

the tree blooming
sea breathing, the beloved son in his cradle sleeping.
Over the hills and skies

on his sleigh the father
the awaited one, made his visitation. Weeks of dreaming
and wondering now

in a box in my hand.
Shoebox size. Not waterwings then or a time machine no
something the size

of a pair of shoes.
Not a pony then or a river canoe. Not a new dress no.
I pulled at the bright bowed ribbons

and little christmas angels
with trembling hands. Underneath the monkey-apple branch
dressed up in baubles and tinsel

and blobs of cotton wool
the sea roaring, stars and the fairy at the treetop
shining

his hand on my shoulder
my mother's eyes on my face two burning suns
piercing my mind and in the box

a doll.
A stupid pretty empty thing. Pink smiling girl. The world
rocked about my head

my face fell into a net
from that moment. My heart in me played possum
and never recovered.

I said I liked the wretched thing
joy broke over my face like a mirror cracking. I said it
so loud, so often

I almost believed it. All that christmas
a shameful secret bound me and the doll and my mother
irrevocably together.

When I knew she was watching
I would grab for the doll in the night, or take it
tenderly with me to the beach

wrapped in a small towel.
At last on the last night of the journey home
staying at a hotel

my mother woke me early
to go out and find the maid. In my pyjamas, half asleep
I staggered out into the dawn

heat rising like mist
from the ground, birds making an uproar, snakes
not yet awake

a sense of something
about to happen under the heavy damp rustle
of the trees.

My feet left footprints
in the dew. When I returned I was clutching that precious
corpse to my chest

like one of the bereaved.
Now I know, said my mother, that although you didn't
want a doll, you really do love her.

I WAS BELIEVED!
Something fell from my face with a clatter—
my punishment was over

and in that moment
fell from my mother's face a particular smile, a kind of
dear and tender curling of the eyes

fell. Two gripped faces
side by side on the floor, smiled at each other
before we grabbed them back

and fitted them with a hollow rattle
to our love. And I layed the doll down in a suitcase
and slammed the lid on its face

and never looked at it again.
And in a sense my mother did the same, and in a sense
my punishment and hers

had always been, and just begun.

4. The Drowned Girl

Christmas morning spring tide the highest of all
mornings, the bringing-in tide
and the waves are sea-monsters flaring

nostrils wide, foam in their teeth
pawing the skies.
A leaf on the wind I am caught at the stairtop

amazed at the slam of water coiling up towards me
afraid and elated as the suck and downpull the outward
roar draws me. An insect on the wind and the garden

all drowned. Drowned the little pathways drowned the gulley
now is a roaring river and the sandunes rise like islands
from the sea that has risen, lifted its head

has come to us driven by the peak of the moon
to speak. This is the day of the christmas service
in the church inland, of christmas dinner

and rich celebrations of eating,
of green mealies and figs for breakfast
and the smell of the turkey roasting

and nuts and raisins in wooden bowls and christmas
pudding. It is all planned, all understood: this day
we obey the good land

parade to church in our white dresses for the blessing
raise our voices in hymns of praise—christ is born
walk in procession past the altar. No one is listening

to the hymn of the sea.
Only Lettie, the nondescript child who appears each year
like a mild weed has heard. The wild sea has taken her –

like a small ship she is riding outward on the current's back
serene as a gull.
O there is a great hullabaloo. The shout has gone up

a girl is drowning! Someone went swimming in the spring tide
is drowning. O why should brave men risk their lives
on christmas morning to save her?

and all is a wild trail of fathers and shed clothes
on the pathway and ropes and frantic wives
down to the massive ocean.

It is christmas morning. Christ is born
Mr Scheepers dare not go in, his heart is not strong
my father and the man from the bakery

plunge into the furious sea. It hurls them about like insects
splits their limbs on rocks and barnacles
flings them soaring on a spray of water, stranded fish

with a roar hurls them vomitting in the sand
their eyes stinging, choking and cursing and bleeding
ears ringing, water water in their heads singing.

O this day the sea is a wild female thing
mad with love for her young will not let anyone near
anyone come in

and the girl sails out without looking back
without a cry
her scarlet bathing cap bobbing in the blue water

like a buoy.
A line of stick figures on the shore
stare at the clear blue horizon.

In the humid afternoon under the trees
under the heavy sun and the silence
a mother has come with her daughter

a new thing
washed up glimmering like a shell. Hair shining
a living thing

she is folded beside her mother
who has brought a thanksgiving to all the brave men and women
who fought to save her:

Here is my daughter.

The mighty sea has returned her from its cold height
to the land. Behold. It clothed her in water, bathed her
in light, brightened her

it has returned her tenderly like a dear
kiss taken, sweetened her like a prayer granted
bathed her in light, in light.

Here is my daughter.

5. The Kiss

Out of a jungle of dreams
at the first creak of morning, the house still dark and
softly breathing

out I went creeping
into the first light of morning where the mighty Puff Adder
at the edge of the verandah

just out of sight
in his rightful place was lying in wait for me
ready to strike.

My first leap of the day
carried me over and beyond him as I turned mid air in my flight
to greet him

he was gone.
O master invisible. Scent of undergrowth
scent of white transparent flowers

sweet and stinging
mist from the tangle of green and fresh sea smell
struck my brain.

Under the luckybean tree
gathering good luck in my basket
I met the Night Adder

master of darkness O beautiful
your fangs inches from my face suddenly flung up mighty
I embrace you

I flee
but the darkness has opened in me, is answering
answering

all night I lie coiled in your exquisite body
my eyes tight shut. If I wake I'll see the slime
at the corners of your lips

you are held in
tight as a spring, a pot of poison. My reflection
moves on your still surface.

Across pale grass the pathway
curves upward innocent as skin towards the drop
the saltclean ocean.

Yet I come.
You exist. Your mate has nested
in my wrist.

Mamba, emperor of all things green
like fire you have slipped between my thighs
at the edge of the world I stand trembling

my father is slashing and slashing
at a wrinkals under the bed with a huge stick. A wild
uncontrollable thing

contracting and flaying the air
cracking and twisting on the floor as we run screaming
from the house as from

a thing immortal.
Who let it in? Its a crisis. We are gathered
to defend something

my mother is nowhere to be seen.
Someone must have let it in. My mother must have let it in.
You give me no rest.

There is something in men's eyes
ritualistic, dangerous, an ancient slit-eyed look
as they file out to hunt you down

my father in the lead
the brave one, his courage on his shoulders
big as a ship.

Yet I come towards you
night after night in my flight from you. You give me no rest.
Your mate has nested in my breast.

And so he came unexpectedly
her eyes half closed not to see
he deceived her. It is his nature.

Two small holes in her calf
two fang marks turning blue. Like a burning thing
she is wildly running

she is mad with pain.
His poison in her body swells out
like an inkfish dying.

Her limbs are turning purple and green
she's an exotic flower, a symphony of pain.
Yet I come.

She is lying under a heap
of poison flesh. All around her, eyes
like trees

bend down and surround her
in a shock of tourniquets and syringes, eyes full of
revulsion, of recognition.

This time we are leaving
for good. I am sent to say goodbye to the sea. Immense and blue
it stretches below me

drowns my crying.
I watch it flow towards me without ending.
I feel dry as a nut.

Kneeling at the water's edge
I gather sea water and salt black weed into a jar
a talisman.

My father packs it up in the boot of the car
and drives us away.
My mother carries the poison of a viper in her vein.

We are survivors
we go out into the wilderness. A microbe
resting on the shore of an artery

might hear the heart booming.

II
Inside Outside

The Cell Attempts To Communicate With The Giant

I believe in you.

A girl in Russia once
could see with her fingertips, being blind.
Her fingers contained

the knowledge of sight.
You exist by deduction. My premise is a kind of
garbled layman's biology

and a conviction you might call
faith or madness
for I sense your presence with senses

I don't know that I have, can never
measure
which is our way of being sure of things.

I know you are there because ears in me
without bone or skin
hear you crying late at night when light points

are visible as stars,
hear a web of pain and confusion in my city
that is your crying

and times I glimpse across the inside of my eyelids
your dreams.
When my world is wrong again it is always wrong

my cells swarm in me like angry
bees, each its own lethal purpose its loud wings
beating, its high pitched menace vibrating

the mysterious ear drum
I don't know for sure that I have.
I believe in you

and I believe the ear drum in you
that might half-hear my high pitched crying
is an ear drum

you don't know that you have.
Only in dreams you might overhear me dreaming.
O my giant

my sorrowful, my alone one
how shall I pass the arteries and the bones
how shall I pass the infinite

distances of space
how will I make you feel my tiny, invisible hands
my infinitesmal wisdom on your vast

too huge to imagine
knot of pain?
Yet I shall cry my message to you

in the incomprehensible whine
of the mosquito and the wind and the snowflake
falling

for you believe you're dying
are courting death while you tell yourself
you believe in survival and

O unlikely
in happiness. There is a cancer is our obsession
cells

hear the man dreaming
form themselves, multiply, build cities in his body
kill him. We are the cancer

your dreams have created
our lives are the fabric of your nightmare
its stiches and bright threads

we are its uncontrollable atoms. Our certain
destruction of you
is the prophecy you half believe in

the pain you have no escape from
the end of everything, the waste, the wild meaningless
annihilation.

O labouring one
dream a different dream. Dream a perfect
golden dream. If I could reach you

I might comfort you
but I'm too small to be even believed in, and I too
in my invisible buzzing life

am locked in my pain, locked in my nightmare, my
prophecy, half hearing
a million tormented cells screaming and screaming

and your breath passing over me in the early morning
is the hailstorm and the holocaust
and the world turning.

The Moment Eclipses

In the gold-haloed face
in the mirror
a shadow traverses the bright
eyeball from within
a planet eclipses my sight
glides slowly, a baleful shadow
across the pale iris.

I am infested with worms
I can hear myself screaming
the larva in the bloodstream
the allergic reaction.
I am shaken with fever
I wake in a rush of darkness
I burrow towards the light.

Mouth dry I cry out for thee
mother, life-giving fly
I am sun with the moon
eclipsing my eye
I am a trick of light on thy fin
I am consciousness
an accidental surfacing
a tumour under thy skin.

Marapper The Priest

I am your priest and your prophet.
May the long journey end
may the ship come home.

Expansion to your egoes may the trailing rot
not get you
beware the wise rats in the sewers

their sharp pink hands on the grating
their infinite vengeance when they pin you to the table
for vivisection, beware

their cruel experience when they knot and cage you
for interrogation.
May the long journey end.

Beware the moths in the ventillation system
beware their quick wings in the delicate
circuiting, beware their deadly

access to the unconscious
as they flutter in your faces, beware their allegiances.
May the long journey end.

Beware the mutants
raiding our barricades with their hideous deformities
beware the outsiders

hatched from pods in the creaking ponics
who live undetected among us
masquerading as men, influencing our children.

May the long journey end.
Expansion to your egoes, a plague on your eyes
we are the refuse

after a catastrophe
trapped in a world built by cruel giants long dead
for a purpose long forgotten.

Turmoil rages in the id
we are besieged from within and without
the crisis was long ago

yet it grows upon us.
Where the ponics slither and rustle in the tangles
and countless small insects gnaw into the silences

our anger bubbles like mud.
To bring frustration to the surface and release it
before it curdles into neurosis

is the work of a priest. We're the sons of cowards
and cowards' daughters anxious to preserve
our present state of misery intact.

May the long journey end.
It is said in the teaching no man's eyes
shall meet another's directly

for the truth never set anyone free.
Expansion to your egoes, the long long journey
has always begun

we forge on without purpose
without direction. Somewhere in this maze of corridors
there must be a control room

there must be a captain
mad, old and mad, O infinite in his madness.
May the long journey end.

We must find him and kill him
we must take the control room, we must create
a destination

may our hands grow quicker
our eyes sharper our arms stronger our tempers fiercer
that we may overcome all who oppose us

may we scatter the entrails of the mad captain
through the length and breadth of the world.
May the long journey end

may the ship come home.

We Embark For Cythera

The beautiful Concubine
is dancing on the grass
touching us and giving us wine

around her beautiful body
the dwarfs playing dulcimers
lick her beautiful breasts

and hide in the forest.
Her pet fawn is nuzzling
by her sweet musty body . . .

Look this is fantasy—we are
serious we are
grown up people.

On the beautiful grass
we are mates, we are *so* clever
talking of philosophy

talking of imprecision
we are *so* witty we have to
laugh we have to

applaud each other
and on a grave we discover an effigy
a man holding an umbrella . . .

Try to think of reality. Think of
dry-rot in the basement think of
the tax inspector.

On the terrible veld
it has rained for a thousand years
and the terrible motor cars are

carnivores they are eating
people. Yes. They are licking their
chops they have warm red blood

dripping down their radiators.
They feed in a pack, it is a fresh
kill, they are feeding like

wolves. Don't be so bloody
stupid it is fantasy I tell you
it is fantasy.

The Lizard Touches Down

A cosmic lizard
has settled on the earth
straddling half the globe with his sixteen
scaly silver legs,
displacing oceans and creating
continents, a disaster of earthquake and tidal
disorder, his immense metallic neck stretching
way out of sight into the heavens.

We shall try at once to destroy him
with our spectacular fire bombs and our nuclear
devices and our scientists
with thrill to the challenge. But if we fail
we shall pray to him.
For bats are flying in the daytime and women
are bringing forth hairy children

and if we fail
we shall beat each other across the head
with sticks, burn each other at the stake
for heretics,
argue into the long night
and drop bright virgins into volcanoes in his
mighty name.
O intolerable! Since he came
the earth has been a convenient
resting place for lizards near the sun.

Inside Outside

1.
Outside the windows there is
nothing.
They are not made of glass they are not
openings.
Outside the door there are no
places
it was not made for opening and
closing.
This room is empty for no memories
hang here
nor is there time
outside this moment in the present.
Outside my inside
I am not sure of who I am, nor who
if anyone
is hiding inside my outside.

2.
We have to find out what we are.
There is a man with a mother and father
steadfast and yielding as two
peach trees,
whose wife is a swift brown river,
whose child is new as the water lily,
who would go as a soldier
would drag a beautiful girl into a barracks
would board up the windows and
lock the door irrevocably

would tear off her clothes with his soldier
hands, would tear her flesh with his
claws, spit in her face and bite off
her nipple in his kiss
his mouth full of blood would
spurt his terrible semen into her body
would writhe and howl with elation
in her agony, in her dying and
he would call it *making love*.

3.
I feel my outer form
flowing away like sand, my limbs begin to
fold and blur, my eyes run together
my torso is contracting
a voice I no longer recognize as my own
a voice gritty with terror
is screaming and screaming
who is this grey shadow, this wiry
mechanical creature, this cowering
crippled thing?

4.
Will the stars steady me in my flight, will
night through the narrow window?
I never know who lurks
behind the gentle face of my greengrocer
what monster may be hiding
inside the outside of my brother with his
strong brown body
what icy, hostile, O inhuman is disguised
in the bland stupid look of
the prime minister.

5.
The voice of the TV announcer
runs smooth as treacle from the sound box
in my room
and on the screen he shows me
a parade of horrors in other places
but never the wounded baby in Ireland
that wakes screaming as nightly soldiers
with blackened faces
search its cot for weapons in streets of houses
that no longer have any doors
for surely we, at least, are safe, are
decent people?
In india the english officer with
delicate hands, ties a man to the barrel of
a cannon for execution.

6.
Inside my outside
I cannot reach, I cannot walk about
touch or see or confirm.
In that darkness the strange dream-creatures
do as they please, cackle and distort.
How many nights have I burst my mind
from sleep with a cry from that other world
that would shrill awake
the dying and the dead?

7.
My outside is plausible as bread,
wholesome and comforting.
My flesh is thickening with age
as it should, I am governed with hunger
in normal human fashion, and a beautiful man
will melt my tangled nerves
into a sweet flow of juices just like
a normal woman.
I believe myself to be a wholly
ordinary human being

8.
yet I have never seen the machinery
that operates my body
I have never tested my skeleton
tasted my blood, I know none of the valves
and intricate water-ways
nor do I have access to a single on-off switch
in the whole wiring system.
I know more about a motor-car engine
though I have inhabited this machine
for thirty years without question.

9.
In trafalgar square
the pigeons and people ripple on the concrete
substantial and alive as
fields of ripe corn:

the national gallery
its belly full of paintings and priceless
art treasures
rises into the close red sky over london
like a hymn.
In the newspapers there are stories of
vietnam and biafra and israel and south africa
and bangla desh and uganda and auschwitz and
stalin and siberia and the opium war
and portugal and greece and spain and
the great potato famine.
The unforgiving sea is peopled with voices
of the captured and the drowning.

10.
If the windows were not made of glass
if the doors didn't open
if there were no past and no future
who would be inside us?
The broken girl staring at the ceiling still
from her torn body is
your sister still
the soldier may be curled in wait and
ready to leap upon her again
from the darkness of my own head.
O my love, what are we left with?
We are witnesses, we are
carbon copies.
We have to find out what we are.

The Giant Sleeps

The giant is sitting on his pebble.
Slightly squint, with a tick in his left cheek
he doesn't see well

yet knows the confusing
tumble of stars
that flick and irritate his vision

aren't the whole universe.
His right hand, convulsively, claw-like
tears at the flesh of his thigh

in savage spasms.
He has pruned his nails down to the quick
has laid gauzes in fine layers

over the torn flesh
has even tried binding the hand like a traitor
to his side.

Useless. It cries and claws
the damage was long ago. His bum aches. Covered in
warts and decomposing skin

it has itched and irritated
as long as he remembers. He can't move — his legs
since that illness he must have had

or was he born like that?
have rested
utterly silent, purple tree trunks

passive, immovable.
His left hand, obedient though ineffectual
wanders over his lost body

like a social worker
patching a little here, comforting there
helpless, full of modest

self approval.
The giant jerks his neck backwards and forwards
in rage. His mind is confused.

Always, the pain in his limbs
confuses him
the darkness of the stars grinds out his aloneness.

He is thinking of dying is thinking of
being saved
is dreaming of a mate, has been waiting

since he was born
since he found himself sitting alone on a pebble
in the swirling universe.

At last the cycle of his endless
sleeping and waking, dreaming and suffering
turns inward on its sunset point.

His eyelids drop, his right hand
convulsing
rips a red streak through the gauzes

his lips form a little song
his genitals swell a little, a moment of joy
sings itself softly open in his groin

and then he sleeps.

What Can We Make To Replace A Man

A bull-doser, a field-minder, two
tractors and a radio-controller
have lost their masters.
There is no longer anyone to work for
anyone to feed.
On a mountainside now they huddle together
high where they climbed
amongst rock and cliff-face, under a million
stars, talking of freedom.
Without hands they clank their metal knobs
against each other for comfort
as dawn precisely comes.

III
The Needy

The Needy

A man in a green cap
has a whip in his hand.
He is a volunteer.
He is whipping another man
dressed in rags. That man
is a thief
is trying to steal a little
rice from a torn sack.
He is starving.
All around them other people
stand packed together
their heads hanging down
their arms extended
like stick insects.
They are also starving
would also steal the rice
if they could get a chance.
The volunteer keeps them back
with his whip.
At last they have loaded the rice
onto a truck. It is being sent inland
to a government official.
He will distribute
a little of it to the needy
of the right religion.
The rest he will sell for a big
profit on the black market.

The starving are trying to climb
onto the ship where the rice is.
The crew keep them back with hoses
and curses. The volunteers in their
green caps keep them back
with whips.
The man from the united nations
is beating his head.
He is disillusioned.
So little is getting to the needy
he cries.

Jane Bird Momentarily Routs the Interrogator At Dawn

Is he clever enough to engage your mind
will your friends with their clever talk
leave him behind?
yes

Is he analytical, mature, full of bright insight
or does he make you feel like a dangerous swamp-land
on the darkest night?
yes

Does he earn money, take care of himself, keep his world
in order, or is he the layabout cuckoo
with a hundred nests?
yes

Is he dedicated? Does he kneel in his work till light
flares round his head, or is his mind
elsewhere?
yes

but a prince. His hands are full of birds
his eyes a clear sky, his love
sunlight in an empty house

ask me that. Yes.

Dilemma Of A Telephone Operator

which department please
    childrens
which department madam
fire police or ambulance
tell me quickly
    the emergency department
yes but which section? tell me
at once what happened and I'll
put you through
    he died whimpering all night
    this doctor won't help him
is he completely dead
    utterly
then you must call the funeral men
they will bury his body
    don't you understand this is
    an emergency
its not our kind of emergency dear
    but you are 999
yes but we have no department as such
to cope with death
    help me
I'm sorry
    help me help me
I'm very sorry. I truly am sorry
    help
O dear try your local church try
the mental health clinic try
the citizens advice bureau

I want him alive again I want
these men to go away
I'm not bloody God. Christ what do you
expect me to do?
if you could see the way he's
lying there without moving
you'd think of something

My Lantern Of Darkness

there's a ring on your finger
big as a moat.

She waits for you, for your returning
steadfast as a baobab, unmovable.

She has drawn from your body's silence
two fine sons, straight

as pine trees. She has planted you
in the future. She is the safe

house you return to.
O the palm-wine drinkard would tap

sweet wine from the palm tree
without damaging it. And you

monsieur the extractor
your quick brown hands that are tangled

with veins, that are deft and knowing
as rats at midnight

gathered with patience you will trick
the frail red flower from the thorn-tree

fruit from the prickly pear
the live heart

from a dying bird. You are maker and predator
I believe you could coax

the equisite skin
from a flaying tiger. It is your work.

It is your function and your dear
stimulation. And I —

I am not of your knotted
and foresty family. You were unleashed in me

mysterious and violent
an eclipse at midday, an avalanche

through a village.
Total. Inevitable. At the shrill praying hour

when black threads are separated from white
in the first light streaks

you leave me for your homeward journey
for your recovering. I am the dangerous

excursion you return from.
She is your rest. The sun rises in her house.

The Last Inhabitant

There is a house between heath and city
where I live.
I own it — have held at bay the long-fingered
bankers and developers and document

grinders for it, stalking through hives of inheritors
like hyenas
wading through ditches lined with the sharp-eyed
rich for it

have tamed the timeless
worms in the beams, rooted out the fungoid
growth in the brickwork
and now its mine.

It is white and still as a shell
and from its high windows the world
seems green and shining.
Tight in my yoke between the widows

in attic and basement I live quietly
but the place seems half empty — a chasm
gapes below me, a devouring pit at street level
darkens my arrival

gnaws at my silences.
The house is waiting for its last inhabitant
a temple with the congregation gathered
before the priest enters

with his warty hands.
I fear that stranger — his purple cassock and his scarlet interiors
his music like thunder and his monstrous singing.

I fear the strangeness of him — his future and
his passion. I see the house
melting into a pool at his feet, see myself floundering

like an emptied goldfish. Often I hear him
pacing my room at midnight, feel his shadow
tracing its net on my sleeping face.
This is no place for him —

its a house of women. Its a house
of pensive Marys. Our anger is not dangerous
our love is reliable
will not curdle in the belly.

I dread his breaking in on us, on prayer
and prophecy.
I dread his coming like the mighty — O furious rushing in of the sea.

A Visit From The Social Worker

Why do you always talk
and never listen?

Mrs Johnson-Bradford's sister used to
talk a lot there were a
lot
of apples in her garden Tom loved
apples
when he was alive.

I have seen the devil.
I have seen him twice.
Today he wore black rimmed spectacles
and sneered
you could smell
hell in him at the other side of the room
hell is full of sneering.

Do you think I'm intelligent
and do you think I'm intelligent
today?
If I tell you I've
drunk all my money again and
borrowed my mother's last quid
again
and drunk it again do you think I'm
intelligent now, this minute?
Do you think I'll be intelligent
tomorrow?

My ambition in life, Sir
is to wash all my dishes and cook
and keep my house clean
every day like my neighbours.

Pamela what did she do
she killed herself on a wet day.
You don't need to jump in public
at certain stations you can privately walk
down from the platform right
on to the rails.

Go away don't
touch me I am
full of anger I am
full of poison
if you touch me
you'll shrivel
go away quickly.

Pamela what did she do
she did it privately on a wet day.
Poor Bernard did it accidentally
choked, all alone in his boarded up room
on a doughnut. I remind everyone
every dinner time. We should remember
ways like that.

We are the real workers you know
the night workers
we work hard every night
I do my foot, and then I do my shoulder
and hold my eyes in so they don't fall out
until morning.
Some people think mad people are lazy
but they aren't they are
full of holes everything
falls out.

I am glad to be mad I am glad to be
mad I am glad to be mad I am glad I
am glad I am glad I am glad glad glad
to be mad.

The Birth

1.
Tonight is the night we are
reborn. This is our second coming.
Silent my mother waits for me
at the end of her long white tunnel.
This time she looks sweet from within.
She is beaming light like a beacon
far out at sea and I am grounded—
soft like a light bulb with moths wings
lighted up around her and I crouch in shadow—
around her people are softened like live
fish in a seashell because she is near them.

I don't believe in her sweetness.
She is unreachable there, she is waiting
for someone else.
For me her shadow on the wall
is more real—is the ache and the absence
huge and threatening a judge to condemn me
is the hanging judge.

2.
Dread gathers in me like lead.
Inevitably it will come
I am floating here—I am peaceful
but this place is not an ending
it is a pit, it is temporary
the bottom
must
drop out eventually.
I curl myself into sullen sleep.

The room is full of people again it is always
full of people being born, full of gasping and
heaving bodies, is full of foetal
desperation.
In her long white light
the earth mother
is giving birth to all her children.
She is chuckling with love.
For each new born, the love chuckle.

I wait in my silent tomb.
I fear the key in the lock and the knitting
needle.
The room is full of children.
Their little faces beam at her like
a thousand sunflowers.
I am so pale. I am invisible and
transparent. Water flows through my body.
My mother has too many children.
I shall be the last again
I shall be again
the turned away one, the left behind.

3.
Time comes for everyone
time came for me
out of my silence. I was
quiet as I could be but the secret
will break, the bottom
will drop
will drop drop drop drop . . .

I shall scream your body down
I shall scream the world down
in the seed in the seed
I am dying I am dying
I shall scream down the sun and the stars
I shrivel out of the universe
in a screaming dark.

Out of the silence her voice comes ringing.
Out of the shrivelled universe
she takes my hand.
Mother. It will begin.
I feel a kind of joy break loose
like a fountain springing
as I kick my way out of you with a howl
of triumph
everything is beginning.

Leper Rejects The Missionaries

priest. hooded messenger in my
territory. night mothman who makes my oneness
glow who lowers huge lights and hungry
lenses down it who tightens

the delicate microphones on it
probing fingers, probing brain, probing
love. and yes the merciless spike
jabs its hunger down the darkness o

sweet secrecy of it, forks and skewers
the pitiful body of it, its small squirming
pink and vulnerable body in its dark
hiding place. o leave me in my aloneness

ding ding ding
squatting in my secret. mothman take away
your torchlight and your spotlight.

and yes it is the same as it has been
and will be again and again. you will not
out me I am buried and missionaries will try me
drop their mines drill and burrow for me and never

not squirm me out through all the soft
centuries. faith will be your undoing ding dong.
think of me not as she but the fruiting body
at the centre, silent fungus of the dryrot

that must in the end crumble the house to
its deep foundations. think of me
as the disease you couldn't cure. infectious.
dangerous. bigger than you and intimately

ruthless. ding ding ding
without thought
without understanding without

malice. this way I am is my function
o go away with your white-coated love and your bright
scalpels, dear father confessor you are
misled. your eyes are round as buttons

your body a deep and warm and all engulfing
refuge in winter, your hurt open and violent
a garden of intricate pansies, each its own explosion
of velvet and purple its upturned quivering face

its own sudden life span and its own
eternal seed. leave me leave me leave me.
she beside you is a ship on the sea. your children
cry and circle like gulls, the sun on their wings

may not be denied. listen to my clapper and my
bells. my wounds are white as milk
listen to the fear of me in your cells

ding ding ding
the fear of me in your cells ringing.
friend. kindness. park—

keeper with your probe and your wide sack
man of god with two tentacles on your forehead
your myriad antenae trembling
leave me leave me

she beside you is a ship on the sea.

The Visit

Silent beside the sunflowers
a lantern beside the sunflowers
light on his hair
forests in his eyes
O fair one is come, my son, *mein herz.*

Silent beside the sunflowers
gathered and still as muscle
his sure hand holds the key
but trembling she opens to him
O she throws wide the doors and the windows
he is the awaited one, the beloved
the youngest son.
Mein schatz, mein herz, alles
ist fertig.

Each day has been
a preparation
and in her house she has become
a curator
shaking out the feather beds, sweeping, with care
the nine exquisite persian carpets
watering the twenty-three pot plants from africa
airing the five bedrooms and
laying out fresh towels.

Each morning, with care
she has set sweet peas in a vase
on each dressing table
dusted five gilded mirrors
scrubbed the italian marble bathroom
swept the inlaid stairs, aired the irish linen
polished the gleaming antique furniture
her old back in the late morning
aching and creaking
in the year's turning.

Each afternoon under the shadow of the mountains
she has laboured in the garden
mowed the lawn and oiled the croquet bats
weeding and pruning she has gladly
bent her old body to the work
dreaming of children
in the year's turning.

Each thorny autumn she has gathered
berries from the woods for jam
each day to be ready she has brought
fresh bread from the bakery on the hill
fresh cheeses and tomatoes and salami
in her wide basket in the year's turning.

Each sunset she has gazed with passion
at her dishwasher, clotheswasher, fridge and cooker
gleaming with whiteness
in the year's turning, in the endless waiting
in the silence of the evening.

Each night when darkness
closes on her like a fist
she has dropped the shutters
locked the fourteen inside and outside doors
whispered goodnight to all the photographs
and the dear possessions
and laid her old body to rest
for tomorrow's waiting
in the year's turning and turning and turning.

Now he carries his long box
carefully up the stairs
and she flutters around him
lighted up with her mother's love
like a meteor in the night.
The table was laid at noon.
The food is in the oven. His shirts
all hanging on the line
his featherbed shaken
fresh flowers in his room.

With sure steps
he moves towards her now
his eyes on her face infinite pits
infinite darkness
and she stretches out her arms towards him
with joy. *Mein kind.*
Alles ist fertig.
Mein schatz, mein herz.

The Death

You said the sheep's dying
is no time to be writing is a time to be
doing something

where we found it bunched at the water's edge
eyes full of darkness, salt foam quivering its fur
and the grey sea sighing —

aaaaaaaaaahhhhhhhhhnngngngngngngng
aaaaaaaaaahhhhhhhhhnngngngngngoooooooooohhhh
aaaaaaaaaahhhhhhhhhhngngngngngngngng

From the city down
we are Mr and Mrs Doing Something
we are calling the policeman.

The sheep must not die by water.
It must die by steaming blood, it must die
protesting

by the butcher's chopper
it must die for the cooking pot not here half frozen
and still as a boulder

the pebbles like so many skulls
acquiescing
wind icy and the salt grey water grey

khaki sea of the dead
of the salt and waiting gathering waters
to fetch it in —

aaaaaaaaahhhhhhhhhhnngngngngngngngng
aaaaaaaahhhhhhhnngngngngngngoooooooohhhhhhh
aaaahhhhhhhhhnnnnngngngngnggng

Stiff now, silt plastering its fur
and the clay cliff sheer
for love of the sheep we crouch, stroke its head

run to the pier and the sleepy harbour
run from the sheep to the shopkeeper. You have given the sheep
your coat, its back is broken.

How you've forgotten the whole world
in this one death
how you fight the whole sea and the sheep's dying

trembling with anger.
The sheep must not die by salt water, this lone sheep
from the cliff fallen

aaaaaaaaaahhhhhhhhhhhnnnnnnngngngngng
aaaaaaaaahhhhhhhhhhhnnnngngngngngngoooooohhhh
aaaaaaaaahhhhhhhnnngngngngngngngng

The farmer has come from his marrows
to the sheep's dying. He is carrying it home on a sack
the saved one

he is bearing it home to the warm fire
a victory
we have cheated the unstitched sighing water

down from the city
and the swell of the dead. Our feet explode on the pebbles
like bones snapping. Before we return

we must climb the treacherous clay
to the high green cliff and the smell of grass
where the lone sheep fell—

aaaaaaaaahhhhhhhhhhnnngngngng
aaaaaaaahhhhhhnnnngngngngngngngoooooohhhhh
aaaaaaahhhhhhhhnnngngngngngng

I Have Seen It Pulsing In Your Veins

I have seen it pulsing in your veins
I have seen it silver all over your hair
and I've felt it perfectly
uncurl in my body
a new leaf uncurls in a room
a bright gull circling
hundreds of miles from the sea.
O mysteriously your skeleton
moves in your body
oceans of little fish lap and flow
in your limbs
and I have never seen you in the morning.

I have seen it in your hands
I have seen it glistening on your skin
I have felt it in my mind unfurling
have bitten into my flesh with pointed teeth
bitterly to control it and hold it in.

I have never seen your bones, nor will I
though they're eternal in you
like rocks and fossils
I have never seen a drop of your blood
nor do I know where you were born
yet I have seen it unfurl over your head
into the evening red with winter
and I've seen it taking root in the room
seeding and rooting in a celebration of green.

Soon it will begin again.
You will live on, and grow old, and your dear
body will bend and wrinkle. On your lips
made small and neat
many kisses hang, still unsung
words wait in your head like seeds
and footsteps
wait in your feet. You have planted your seed also
in the belly of your son and your daughter –
you're forever a garden
and though your absence
fills my house
I give you back the sun and the wide night now
my precious one.

Passing Through

In a rugged barn of a house in nottinghill
you had taken possession
like a field mouse, building a nest for yourself
inviting your friends in.

In a corner of the basement we sat huddled together
our coats and boots tightly gripped around us
your things strewn a little on walls and floor in
a gentle statement.

Suddenly restless I wandered off
and up the dark stairs, peering into room after empty room
all dark, with night showing through bare windows
like squares of grey cloth.

The house was a hillside, belonging to nobody
all the past inhabitants now scattered footprints –
a patch of silver and pink wallpaper;
a careful light fitting where a bed must once have been.

It was bone cold. In its heavy row of houses it was part of
hundreds of years of brick and timber and tile in the night –
it seemed no more a house than a cliff might be
to a nest of starlings

nor a human shelter but a part of the timeless
landscape of london where people might be born and grow old
and pass without anything changing. A wry comment
on a board outside said SOLD

as a flag somewhere on the moon declares it
American Land.
Wandering through it was like a pilgrimage and in a room
somewhere near the roof I found

another human, huddled in his dressing gown
writing a letter to his love at a rickety table. He let me in
and on his narrow mattress we mated
and he told me I was shiny and sparkly and I told him

he was dark and secret as a night river thus telling each other
about ourselves. Sleep in that room didn't come easy for me
I was half on the floor and stiff with cold and the pillow
though filled with straw felt like

a bag of pebbles. Whenever I begged him to wake
he half mumbled in his sleep that he had to
work tomorrow
so I lay and watched the red morning gathering among rooftops

and pigeons, like us, resting
and the signs of other pilgrims who had passed and in one corner
his rough bag of clothes and his bag of cameras in another
his special claim to being *someone*.

At last we got up, avoiding eyes, nuzzling each other for warmth
out of kindness, knowing each other as strangers.
A note from you left in the corner where you had been
told me that you'd moved on

and your mate, on his own now
wandered down the stairs in a big black beret and cloak
theatrical still, like a character from Dostoyevsky
off to buy fruit at portobello road

with Ophelia on a lead now you were gone.
Sweet girl, open still as a field without hedgerow or harvest
you are nearer completion than any of us
squatting in our warm houses, dreaming of permanence

and ownership, sticking our flags
into walls and doors and windows and gardens
into each other
into the high moon.

for Sylvia

IV
Graces

Grace to the Sculptor

Out of clay you formed me
smooth and symmetrical, two sides
identical
matching hands
matching feet
matching eyes
matching breasts
and my orifices neat
down the centre of my stem.

This time I am balanced with precision
will not bend and crack
splitting open.
Like thee I am made
for knowing and making, like thee
for loving and breaking.

Grace for Potato

For the faithful potato we praise thee.
O firm friend, who made potatoes
who made their solid white bodies
their roundness and their strong brown skin
who made them for winter
after you'd made butter, who made their
many eyes, and their full comforting bellies.
You made the potato
on a day when you felt indestructible
when the world's hunger was to be once and for all
cured, under the earth you planted such an abundance
such an overwhelming store of contentment
for the good and faithful potato root
we praise thee, praise thee, praise thee.

Grace for Snow

I prayed to you for sleep, for silence
from the night-voices and peace
from the night-faces.
You sent cloth in thick folds to cover and close
the shiny black eye of the night's window.
I prayed to you for a blessing, for grace
from the slow scream of the city's sorrow.
You sent snow.

Grace for Tomato

For the frail tomato
we praise thee.
In times of fasting
she lies gleaming on the plate
substantial as glass.

In times of plenty she is
blood of the soup
delight of the stew
good friend to onion
a balm to chile and sharp green pepper
astringent cleanser of the greasy
fried egg, that pensioner –
that irritable hunchback
nestling in his symbol
smug as a cliché.
Tomato is his protector.
Tomato is his patron.

From her powdery vines
from her hot fields and distant islands
she comes in shining.
For the frail tomato
rose of africa
we praise thee.

Grace for The Clear Water Of The Fountain

On a stone hillside you were meditating.
The sun you had made, like a warm
friend's hand
had gloved itself behind a bank of clouds.
The white sheep you had made, like
boulders were resting in the valley.
The air you had made, smelling of silence
of the end of summer
hung motionless about you, hardly breathing.
You were thinking about the loneliness of
completion
when suddenly you heard singing and dropping
your big thoughts in a heap
a boy again, you were
leaping from rock to rock, laughing and
calling out loud, your cries echoing
eyes stinging as you rushed to meet it
where it came
springing from the earth like a million
tiny wild angels
singing, singing.

Grace for Sex

Where I stood on my high beach
waiting for the tidal wave to roll in and consume me
and he washed up at my feet like an old memory
you
little psychopath
little wild god of the swamps and thickets
crept up on me from the land like a small mammal.
You were silky as the slime of a snail
your body translucent and smelling of flowers
your seaweed hands and your laughter
an orchestra of flutes in the muscles of my groin.

Ungovernable one now morning is gathering
I hear you curl yourself inward to sleep again, warm
furry and purring, inscrutable
and we find ourselves strangers
tangled together on the floor in a chill squat
in nottinghill, on a mattress of straw.
My big truths all convoluted I lie smiling to myself
mute and smiling.
Little god you have washed me
clean as a grapefruit
I acknowledge thee.

Grace for Death

Something had changed, I smelled it
instantly
leaf of the bluegum breaking
leaf of the lemon tree unfolding
and the claw in her chest had unclenched
her face let go
its itchy needing to know look nor did she mention
Klee or Picasso.

You silky still and glistening
on her unfinished dreams
she let me sing wildly on and on about
saving something
waving towards me as one who had known you
long and deeply
all she had kept to give me gone
but love.

Lord of darkness
may I live lightly
in knowledge of thee, build my years
wisely, thy seed in me
take thee at last for a lover in my body and
go with thee gladly
where everything is an opening
in thy strange kingdom.

for Inge

Grace for Joshua

Night at high tide
my heart crashing about in my chest like
a trapped animal

my body buzzing with panic
whispering fish faces of the dead with
decayed eyes

the drowned house hissing with emptiness
a prowl of gloved feet by my bed
and the dread of meeting

you Joshua

snug as an old shawl
little hot water bottle, purr
stretch your soft coiled body slow and heavy

as I press you to my throbbing
your eyes unblinking still green pools
contemplate me

still me
and you make sleepy whimpering noises like
a milky child.

Grace for Hyacinth

In my new gold room
where the winter sun swam
like a shoal of glad dolphins
and everything was gleaming
you grew like a dancer.
For three days I watched you
flowing open
unfolding yourself green and white
the music of your dance
just out of ear range
humming in my body, the sweetness of
your breath
kissing and kissing me.

Praise the white flower who
mothered thee praise
the brown bulb that housed thee
praise the green moment
that gave thee birth
and all thy life
hyacinth.